PRAISE FOR
CAN YOU SIG

"A heady mashup of Black pop culture, geekdom and an homage to Caribbean musicology and lore. With such alluring titles as "Cthulhu Asks for Kendrick Lamar's Autograph" to "The Metaphysics of a Wine," O'Brien interweaves humor, politics, beats, rhymes and bacchanal with the fantastic and the cosmically horrific—giving us something literary, lyrical and amazingly unique. Allyuh gonna like this!" —P. Djèlí Clark, author of *A Master of Djinn*

"The black experience in verse with all the beauty, the humor, the terror, and the resilience. Brandon is a song at the intersection of hip hop and horror that challenges the soul and demands to be heard." —Maurice Broaddus, author of *Pimp My Airship* and *Buffalo Soldier*

"The perfect pairing I didn't know I needed. Drawing on eldritch and hip hop influences, O'Brien melds the two with a skilled hand, incorporating the best of both to speak on racism, family, misogyny, climate change, and more—much of it heartbreaking, all of it true. Reading like an album, it takes you on a journey as he remixes topics and revisits themes. Can You Sign My Tentacle? booms, whispers, and everything in-between, and O'Brien perfectly sticks the landing, with the last line of the collection lingering for days afterward." —Jordan Hirsch, author of "The Last Bookseller of Saint Paul" and other short fiction and poetry.

"Dreamlike, visceral, and emotionally moving. An intoxicating poetic journey and a heartbreaking ode casting your fave hip-hop artists juxtaposed with chilling and beautiful imagery through the haunting lens of tangible pain, loss, grief and love." —Tlotlo Tsamaase, author of *The Silence of the Wilting Skin*

"All the poems in O'Brien's collection, like tracks in a poetic album: entertains, amuses, enlightens and inspires. More than anything else, his Author's Note is the perfect ending for this Album of the Year for me, sharing the poet's journey in the realm of science fiction, the impact of Cthulhu mythos and the relationship to Blackness & racism. I will sign any tentacles he waves in my direction."
—Linda D. Addison, award-winning author, HWA Lifetime Achievement Award recipient and SFPA Grand Master.

"Can You Sign My Tentacle? is a book of cosmic horror poems that takes the genre and its racist roots and flips it. The description reads "Lovecraftian-inspired nightmares are reversed as O'Brien asks readers to see Blackness as radically significant." This refers to the significance of continuing to struggle and survive against huge structures of power trying to destroy them. The idea seems to be that the horrors aren't nearly as awe-inspiring as the struggle. Imagine, if you will, a human standing before Cthulhu shouting "I'm still here, you big slimy fuck!" —Land of Chel

Can You Sign My Tentacle?

Brandon O'Brien

This is a work of fiction. All of the characters, organizations, and events portrayed are either products of the author's imagination or used fictitiously.

CAN YOU SIGN MY TENTACLE?

Edited by Holly Lyn Walrath.
Cover design by Trevor Fraley.

Published by Interstellar Flight Press
Houston, Texas.
www.interstellarflightpress.com

ISBN (eBook): 978-1-953736-05-5
ISBN (Paperback): 978-1-953736-04-8

First Edition: 2021

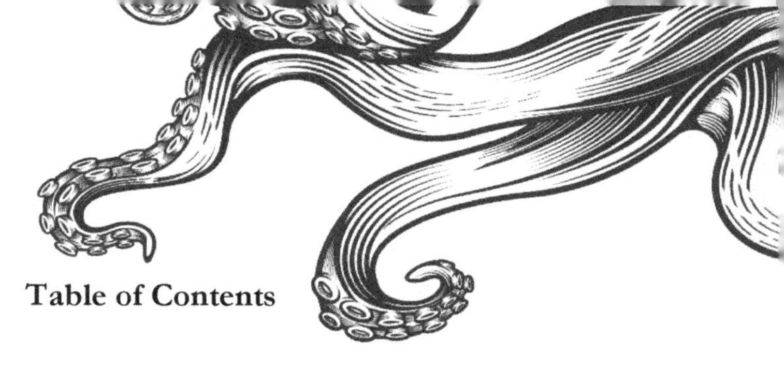

Table of Contents

Hastur Asks for Donald Glover's Autograph

a‖

In his house at Stone Mountain, real hip-hop Gambino
stays woke.
In floaters, he can see spacetime on opposite
ends of a line of scrimmage, watch them collide into
nebulae
to the point where he can't even find himself out of that
mess.
He doesn't really know sleep. There's too much to know.
Before the entourage parks outside the 2013 version
of Sway In The Morning, he's already seen how it all
middles.
His gaze collides with the higher homes so hard he sits
in the studio sleepy-eyed and static. He has no problem
telling
folks they will all die someday. He gives away
Nostradamus
in thirty-two bars. He donates his barstool philosophy in
place of a chorus.

b‖

The other realm is lit like neon purple-green on sparklers
while the eldritch Elders sup sauce and complain about
their complicated family lives when Donald Glover in
a maroon cape floats by on grace. The Peacock King
himself flags him down before he can disappear,
and goes, 'aren't you in the wrong place?'
'Bino says, 'Nah'. Hastur goes, 'I don't think you wear that.'
'Bino says, 'I wear whatever, man.' When Hastur
asks for an autograph for his shapeless niece, the pen
bursts vertices of truth all over the girl's wings,
but she plays it off like it was nothing. They gawk at
the dude like he's so huge, his own orbit's unbeatable
even by apathy. He'll forget their faces shortly. The idea
of it will probably vex them all so much. He'll take
the nihilism with him, though.

c||

If 'America' is in the title, it's documentary.
First off, the man in that footage has no name,
or is named 'Hopelessness', or is named 'Legacy',
or just answers to hawk-cry. That ain't Troy.
No matter. Both of 'em lucky to be alive,
but one got on a boat, allegedly transcended all of this.
The other dreamt tendrils of things it shares a name with
until anxiety turns solid inside. The other tried to film
what he saw, but the lens kept finding things to laugh at
no matter the angle, even the bodies. The camera turned
and opened its jaw on him, shattered onto him like a
lightbulb,
and the truth, frayed, started screaming curses. No, that
ain't Troy. But he's in the frame somewhere.

d||

Twin Peaks: The Return, Part Eight, 'Gotta Light?'—
something bursts in the desert and gives birth
to darkness that waits to be consumed fresh.
Crawls into ears like lullaby, crawls between lips
like offering. Takes advantage of those who sleep.
Goes looking for fragile light to try to eat.

Atlanta: Robbin' Season, Episode Six, 'Teddy Perkins'—
Darius just wanted to pick up a sweet piano.
Turns out that goodness is often light-sensitive.
Turns out that darkness leaves all of its windows open
and makes lullaby out of everything. Turns out there's
a duality in everything, and there's blood
everywhere. Light takes its own life before it can be food.

Both episodes kill fearsome dread with humility.
Both tell you to run from what lingers in
wooden rooms.
Both are bright and odd, end in flat light burst.
And plus, Rotten Tomatoes loves them both.

ell

You ask him about chaos in front of the late-
night studio audience. His autograph changes
shape before your eyes. You ask him why he's so
nonchalant about death. He reminds you
nothing is more freeing than knowing the cosmos
isn't attached to you. "It feels like floating,"
he says. "I wish I could still have that,"
he says. Uneasy, the late-night host tries not
to look one tall audience member in the eye:
mustard coat, wriggling sinew, all grins and hollers.
The host asks, "Why can't you have it?"
"The cosmos just won't leave me alone."

because who she is matters more than her words

there is a wolf prowling
in the stalks outside a black woman's
Twitter profile, gnawing at
the bark of unsheathed pencils
and waiting to leap

at an unsuspecting neck. moonlight
strikes the head of a rocket statue to trigger
the pack, they howl and scrape
at the spines of scary galleys
with names they gutturally mispronounce for fun

but the heroine of this story just
takes her first draft and rolls it up,
throws the dusk-to-dawn lights on
outside the house that knows itself
and swats some of the tykes on their noses

till they scatter. her neighbor puts up
a warning: the residents here ain't the ones.
the next HOA meeting makes a fence of bodies,
gathers its own nets, immunizes its own from fatal ideas,
puts buckshot in the barrels of their fountain pens.

we will hear about another pack before day even breaks,
best believe, but even our kids will know, will put
pebbles in their slingshots as warning. they will
tell stories in the cafeteria about how their mothers
were good with the blades of pens,

how they learned how to hold one early,
how nobody could ever tell them nothing 'bout who they were.
and one night, when harvest night calls for starving wolves,
those children will reach for their mother's weapons,
and cast light like there is no night.

Cthylla Asks for Drake's Autograph

The gurgling girl runs into Drizzy as he shoots up
like a meteor through the universe. He's in a hurry,
he ain't got no time. He doesn't hear her scream.
He barely hears her scream. When he hears her
scream, he puts on his light-skinned voice, says
he's focused on this grind, on feeding his day-ones,
how an autograph isn't the same as work.
She says she's just asking for one minute,
she's been listening since he turned stellar,
come on, man, just one autograph.
He scrapes through her left wing with a ballpoint pen.
She's going on about how she loves that
he's amorphous like she is, one moment he's
down for the settle-down and the next he's soft breath
tumbling out of the window and gone,
one moment he's hard like bricks in flight and then
his voice is brown rum through a buzzing phone line.
Drizzy nods, says thank you, tries to head back up
up and away but the girl won't stop talking about
a future the boy didn't prophesy himself.
She blinks all eight orbs in a cascade
and watches him flutter into strobe-light burst
till the street turns quiet.

the repossession of skin

you're glad to have a uniform, right?
cool.
  find another. some of us live in this one.

you came to the wilds, you say—
'your motherland', you tell me,

hands clasped, grinning like the devil.
aren't you so damn lucky?

it's like your grandparents spat on the map
just in time for you to 'teach me about my roots'.

the same ones I want to choke you out with?
take that costume off. please.

you have a 'name' now, something
'important'—like 'Phantom' or 'of the Jungle';

you ever notice how it's always in Imperial English?
but then again, I also hear

your cousins have gotten good at
literally stealing christenings from other mothers' mouths.

take that off.
really.

someone has to sleep and wake in that skin.
you're just sweating and masturbating in it.

okay. I know. maybe we trade, then?
maybe I go study under a white master

to perfect the art of colonialist capitalism;
maybe one of my buddies

falls off the side of a mountain in the Deep South

and stumbles into the way of the Colt Python

and we fight hordes of TV execs
who throw milquetoast casting calls with lethal force

and we win by stabbing each
of them in the eye with our fountain pens

and we peel their pale exteriors with our hands
and bite into whatever wicked pulp rests beneath

and we get whole seasons of ourselves
and neither of us gets written out

and our bodies still belong to us
and our bodies never forget the sound of our voice.

that show is much mightier
than you stripping us of our layers,

throwing the thinnest of them
over you like a nightgown

and dancing in the streets
insisting you've discovered something.

we won't fucking ask

again.

The Sailor-Boys

We is some rebels, yes.
We does still sneak out the window
close to midnight with we sailboards
under we arms, scaling the outer
island walls to ride the winds.

Up here, we ibis-free, the bellies
of we boards scarlet, or yellow
like kingbirds, cutting the gale
like skipped stones could split water.
We is some *aves*, yes,

watching cormorants stain in the
blackwater beyond the beaches
where rigged exploitations did catch fire
but couldn't have enough water to douse it.
We is some blessed ones, yes.

My mother did say we was once like
the black(-gold)-and-white(-collar) world of the developed,
all of their bigger pictures with no solutions,
but we let all our colours fly. Like
us boys doing now before sunrise,

we is some fresh starts, yes.
We does soar over sighing tragedy,
the heaving high tide of Mama Dlo short of breath,
and laugh, cheer the wind on as we float.
We is some rebels, yes.

Lovecraft Thesis #1

(*Lupe Fiasco's Food and Liquor*, Track 2)

we have always concerned ourselves
at core with the same element:
the real. the act of documenting truths
some may never find the synaptic fortitude
to fathom:

the fathoms of the star path above
the fathoms of the middle passage beneath
that life is more than lilied assumptions
that a story can be stored in goatskin
or that it carries petabytes
to be unlocked via psychic probe
or verbal passcode

unraveling is a course of our flow
that which stores us is undone
only we get to record the path
in curling fists of language
if you can't make sense of what
the rhythm of time seeks to say
then it wasn't for you

postcard 20xx, where there are no dirges

the streets can't help but sing our names back to us. it sounds like a
Mother's Union choir rising out of the mango roots, a well
geysering with love. every tanty's voice was a procession orchestrated

to keep the block stone-still, to remind us of when the lapels would plot
to kick the dust out of the pavement, to paint it chaconia by
at least six-thirty, to write the words SOMEBODY CHILD in chalk, certain

of the justice of wild and swinging pain. i remember when the whole gang
of boys on my block come to see the ancestors off, our mothers and the leaders
of every mass muttering under their breath, Lord, make sure to take them in,

the streets are a frigid region. we sing every name, craft Johnnie flambeaux, the
ice boxes burst open with juice and rapid comfort for the aches, we slap hope
against we thighs to keep the rhythm as your granny dance in the kitchen to

the sound of your father's name. all of us boys remember the night we get
our mother scared the first time, her writing our names everywhere, whispering it like a national
anthem into the corners of the house, hoping the bricks would lend us support

sometimes my brother would venture outside our garden's edge into the

castle that the past had built to store the children that they didn't plan
to make soil of right away. he would stare at it for hours, try to
pull loose bricks out hoping he would destabilise
the wall, say he was just making sure that all of the
spirits got free. he said he hoped they swam the whole sky above the country,

that nothing kept them still but their mothers. he and
the others wrote the names of the men without children, put
the papers together as kites, let the wind take each by law.
every evening he found a new one, gazette paper abiding,
he made sure the evening got all its forsaken citizens
before our mother called us back in

for dinner. And he'd eat like for all of history's harm's
done, he let some names live forever, in our mother's way.

hunting dog

in the dim
the name on my box
is of the expected dead
missed and still invisible

don't study how easy
they rise up foam of spit
of drunkard journalists
bylines growing hot

their names fresh-wet
on the door of my casket
once, it said Sean, and
muddy water filled my mouth

silence smelling of sugar and blood—
it said Keyana, cloth dragged
from my chains, I smell
sweat and tears, muffled agony

rings through my ears—
then Dana, and the links
round my hand electroplated,
judgment-light pours out stigmata.

and each morning I must bear the
ignoble sacrifice of waking
sober-faced, no wolf-teeth,
no quenk-head, justice does wait

for nightfall for me to hold your sins,
Simon helping Trinidad to bear them,
listening to them wail on my back,
what kind of monster?
                    indeed.

me, chained, a thing with fangs—

a hunting dog, with birds on my back
—and then, become so cursed
as to look like you.

let me tie you to their names.
smell and sip their unmakings.
                    your blood does taste better chilled anyway
                    but you better learn before I consume.

Hastur Asks for Lord Kitchener's Autograph

Far stranger things have revealed themselves
in the spaces between the mundane and the much-more-than,
where bees unlock voix celeste,
where the dead just want All Fours partners.
He done learn sometimes the unknown
just need someone to sing in their direction.
When the guest holds out a tendril,
say 'my daughter loves your work',
Kitch already grinning.
Whatever words share in this moment
I could only believe:
song-stories from new and wilder places
trade in the breaths between uncapped marker
and stained vellum skin. Hastur nods.
How often do you get the chance
to share a moment this grand?
It must have stunned him to pure silence
thick enough to be mistaken
for dread.

the lagahoo speaks for itself

you think I is the monster?
nah—I is just a funeral procession
with canine teeth.
I does keep the lists when
you forget your children's names,
I growl them low in the night.
I am a rabid memorial—
one that does snatch the mournless from their beds,
one with breath that stink like remorse
I know the scent of every dead girl's close male relatives
I could sense the sour of trigger fingers
in the alleys at the edges of hotspots
and the sticky-sweet of six figures
in the conference rooms with the hotshots
and all of them left residue on the dead
still fresh-wet on the bones,
stones slick with your wickedness.
you think I is the monster?
I don't eat my young.
I will, however, feast on the
tight-fisted and apathetic how I please,
calling their names over the dinner plate,
breaking all your headstones into my palms,
picking my teeth with the memory of your name.

Lovecraft Thesis #2

(*Splendor & Misery*, Face B, Track 2)

Violence makes good background noise
for anything. Even for knowledge.
People suffer for knowing all the time
in your stories—you know, the ones where
something shrouded in shadow stalks the
corridors between neon and dancing
with its eyes on everything gentle
and its tendrils on everything glimmering.
How dare you tell me this is somehow
unfathomable?

What is the block, child?
What is it if not the night
turning liminal, sliding into the dark upper sea
where we hold back knowing?
It batters the bones of things
that want to see beyond their horizon,
it is the storm that walls off the new edge of the world,
the barricade that blurs treasure or threat
outside your reach.

And yet you still wish to know.
To venture beyond fear's camp.
To lose your mind in its gyre.
The corner will cry in its usual way,
cry copper and betrayal,
cry having faith in what you know,

but you will cross the threshold anyway.

That Business They Call Utopia, Part Two

I've witnessed that business they call
building a utopia for so long,
higher up the Atlantic where yearning to breathe
free meets committal at the gate.
I've been so frightened, friend.
They say over here that we catch the other nations'
colds across the water in the storms, so

often I wonder how to ward them off:
what warmth but a hearth of good-mornings,
what vitamins but the scent of fruit
from neighbors. I've witnessed this
utopia-building business bake bricks from
screaming, friend, and I've seen the masonry
trade grow on it, shake down big spenders

for iron, for foil tents, for rations,
for tears with which one churns cement.
We keep saying that this is like a fantasy novel,
the ones where there are great houses or great cities
or great castes, the ones that cast us castaway,
the ones where the aching children free the phoenix
from their ribcage and torch it all.

We keep saying it's a poorly written one,
because look at the dialogue, look at the
mise-en-scène, and look, there are so many children,
but where are all the flames? And friend,
I have seen the utopia business pick up
outside your house, I've worried about the shape it takes,
worried about whether the scenes resemble

the shouting on Market Street
or the shouting on Tragarete Road,
whether kingdom's copper foot
lifted from the waters of war
and crawled to the shore with
all its crows. What else can my soft hands

give but worry? And is saying so even
my right? But if the stories taught me
anything about how to prepare
for this moment, it's this: everyone has a little
fire to spare, a neighbor for whom to share it,

someone for whom hope is the phoenix
still waiting, pecking at our skin while we call it fear.
And you can have my fire, but first,
have this other thing:
I love you, friend, and I love you more with each flambeau-
word your tongue waves for your street,
with each phoenix-word as you throw the weighted
consonants against the glass walls of this.

Take both. The stories say when we can spare just those,
one beside one, two beside two, there's no wickedness our
clasped hands can't split, even when
beside is an island in the other direction
where you cannot hear my heartbird
crying out to yours, be safe, be safe,
but burn those bastards' pillars down.
And it sings, it sings
the song the poems say it would sing,
for you, friend. You.

Birth, Place

I made this land myself.
I put dirt in my own
mouth and hoped it
would mature; you made
      manure of the bodies
of our mothers, asked
us to chew the remains,
and on our tongue they
whispered, *Babalú-Ayé,*
make my children potters

of a planet, give them
farmers' hands, and turn
their captors into meat
for sand.
      I baked the
soil myself, let the dough
of it roll in my first language
so it would taste sweeter,
coated it in seeds of faith and made
heat of my heart enough
for home to cake around me.

Your legacy's already drowned me,
you dragged me along water not
fit for baptism and my brothers
swam anyway; cold wind
cracked their bones outside your windows
and our daughters grinned
and took it. We asked Yemọja
what rain would work to water
a home, and she said
Whatever sea is in your mouth
will season your final island.

Know that my landlords are
greater than yours. I
made this land myself,

a recipe written in the heavens
and taste-tested by ancestors
and peppered with ashes.
Shade will one day grow
in the place where your father's
bones once called me low.
I will plant a time I cannot see
for children I will not know
among those bones,

and what grows, laughing,
will not be as easy to pluck
as I once was.

Cthulhu Reminisces Upon The Mighty Sparrow and Lord Melody's Autographs

Sometime in the late fifties
I was just lingering in someone's fear of flying
when I noticed them: rum in their cups.
huddled over scribbled lyrics and laughing
from Piarco to New York City
on their way to let Belafonte plant calypso in the Garden.
I think Melody just figured me ugly,
some more kind family's well-meaning man,
offered a tea-warm smile as his pen skipped paper.
Sparrow dances a marker over the
corner of the sleeve of *The Slave*
without a glance. Not like he was being cold;
under his breath he mutters how he's
tired of obeah following him.
I thank them, they nod short,
and for a moment, they fell quiet.
Then their muse's fury flares anew
in tighter whispers—before I
could lean to sneak a sight of the results,
Mister Francisco hums a tune
and the shadow I came through starts to close...

postcard 20xx, of our garden and beach

a thousand sunrises after the miasma, the sea was a glass wine wind, but
we also had other things. when we could dance on soil again,
we made dances of everything. you could see it
in a child's firm touch of their parent's hand, in the infinite closeness of lovers' lips, it is

indomitable space, ruled by wild poinsettia and paphinia cristata, thwarting what is difficult.
the navy blue lapels used to stop us dancing, tanty used to say. they'd wait for
a boy hued like me in his school uniform, or any neighbour too small for the

shirt on his back, shout why he was greedy for sun. she say they police
the rations of breath itself to
each of we by the way the mountains intervene

the wind. but that was a thousand dark clouds ago. because
my tanty and her tanty chanted our names on the wind, it
is owed us well. we water the green-streets, each living pavement is

all of ours by the sun, never begging any of us shade in private,
no longer a plantation-right, or a baton's secret guarded property.

Cthulhu Asks for Kendrick Lamar's Autograph

Each sheet fills with sound,
funk throttles the margins' throats shut—
finally something is incomprehensible
to this, to the size of stars.
Something worth recognising.

It is noisy, it clashes
with every corridor of doubt,
it claims the empty space with a
pompous shout.

Maybe even too pompous—
it cheers, takes new names
and dances in the step of the old ones, too,
it grasps, it owns,
it turns swift and has a handsome dip
to it. Every curve insists.

It insists.
It isn't always right, but it insists.

Perfect.

Young Poet Just Misses Getting MF DOOM's Autograph

I just wanted to ask about the mask.
I just wanted to ask about having a spare self,
a decoy for before worries. I wanted to ask about
leaving a talented neighbor my cloak to bear
the burden of my heavy lurid verses while
you're elsewhere sculpting the scheme in the
next scene. I just wanted to ask about the name.
I could never imagine being
the lord of so any realms, with so many realms
within me fighting to escape all the time. Not escape—
debut. I just wanted to ask about the mask.
I wanted to ask about being a whetstone
and a blade all at once, steel against steel,
tongue as a stun gun weaving words for the young ones,
running with homespun puns willing worlds never undone
I just wanted to ask about the name,
the pride in becoming the villain
in places where that was all we could excel in

but I never quite got within autograph distance,
and that's fine, maybe in another moment.

Kanye West's Internet Bodyguard Asks Hastur to Put Away the Phone

Damn, this thing just
loves to find something that means something
so it can swallow it in swirling jaws and erase it all.

He was just walking down a Twitter feed late one night
looking ironically for a hamburger
and he met the mess rushing upward on the sidewalk,

swearing across the cold while some other VIP walks away
chuckling. He takes out his phone to catch Ye
in the entire internet. He spins a slick caption

underneath to snare a couple likes as they crawl upwards.
Hastur shouts *Worldstar!* out of sight, a gleeful
judgment-sound, lucky no one will hear

until it fades into the midnight. The whole block
puts a part in their mouths, laughs their little laughs
with their mouths full, *oh he so crazy!*

When I see it, I remember nearly passing out
with my own desire to disappear. I remember
the sidewalk of my own timeline rising up to meet my nose

and strangers kneeling to ask me if I was dizzy,
bringing tepid water, wiping my bloody forehead.
I wonder if Ye brought any friends with him to the club.

I wonder why no one's taken Ye to bed. I wonder
why no one's taken Hastur's phone. I wonder why the street
is always so full when Worldstar and always so empty when
world-weary.

The video stops trending eventually. Maybe we'll
think about it so we can redirect our
          judgment, feel better right after feeling bad.
          But the video never comes down.

the one

830, 831, 832, 833—
on his digits he can
see the crumbs of past attempts at family.
He licks the strawberry stains
and lists them in turn:

- rejection via drowning at a river in Estonia
- so many silver baubles as he wooed British royals
- a dozen unique moments when
  men wanted blood more badly than he did.

In a new almanac flyleaf he scribbles
I keep counting on the One—
952, 953, 954, 955, nine-fif—
teeming with restless numbers,
he goes into the university racket,
slings pure uncut figures,
counts the hairs on students' heads for boredom,
knows each test-catalysed yawn or sigh in a tally,
tries to keep his failed love number small:
962 times I thought I'd found the One.

Too many years meet each other
and concentrate into indefinite
infinity, the kind of
thing he hates not fathoming.
The bookstore owner is also an infinity:
she resembles that one free belle
when he nursed wounds in Georgia,
her giggle takes him back to
a brook in a countryside he barely
remembers but closed his eyes to hear
each drop.

She is briefly
the only thing that makes sense.
One whole thing *or*
a collection of points in space *or*
{all the fears you can have in your body | those fears <
boundless joy} *or*

P(reciting an old poem he hadn't heard
since Dickinson waved the page at him herself > the attacks
that come to her in the middle of the night sometimes when
the wrong song plays on the radio)—

they touch and
the only thing that counts is her.

What were the odds?
She's read enough lifetimes to
feel just as old as he does.
In the small spaces between lines of postmodern poetry
he can count entire continua
clashing for a chance to sound.

Cthylla Asks for J. Cole's Autograph

ask a creature of contradiction
and unfathomable mathematics
about the paradox of
how does a man better himself
in the same sentence he uses 'bitch'?
preceding praise for promiscuity.
maybe you're only saved from the mayhem
by thinking from the basement.
Cole slides out the front of a Bentley—
rented; true power is spending money
on transient glamour—and their eyes
meet in the meat of the avenue.
he ain't headed nowhere in particular
she's in the area for him
you can hear bluebirds somewhere
she can still unravel the fact that
he says the word *bitch* eight times
in the first five minutes of meeting
two of those times he whines awake
that he should stop
but they aren't even the last two
she doesn't care
if anyone needs rescue last, it's her
she smiles at every scratch of wit
asks coquettish for an autograph
a pic for the 'gram
he takes a blue sharpie to her chest
barely smiles into the camera
someone shouts across the street
that she should stay away from him
he waves the shout off as haterade
as the girl-god distends her jaw

    don't save her

Lovecraft Thesis #3

(*There Existed an Addiction to Blood,* Track 12)

The fact is, you are just a chalice
for the ritual of melding truths.
Your ribcage holds them badly,
but you are.

Because of this, the death
your poorer historians have stored to ink
is never the true suffering.

It is always forgetfulness.
Don't even let them offer you the instability
of your walls of thought.

You can let each fear of forgetting
fall against your tongue crimson like wine,
like nebula dervishes rich with dreams,
and in you is a chalice for them all,

and you go running toward the fear
and drink deep,
get lost in them,
you love the way control fades.

You are less fragile, then,
than you suppose.

The Metaphysics of a Wine, in Theory and Practice

whereas many more presumptuous
theories suggest an interpretive dance
in five deliberate movements (Marling &
Batmanglij 2017) or else a general physical
denial of body through writhing-as-dance
under strobe-lit dark,[1]
the newly discovered academic consensus is that
multidimensional transcendent astral travel
is only possible through
wining

the dancehall take me
to Heaven last night
and I wish I coulda stay

the adequate performance of gyratory sublimity
is capable of euphoric states, restoration of
stamina, and treatment of anxieties,
but at supercritical depths
a wine has the potential to bestow
near-preternatural consciousness to the
recipient (Ziggy Rankin 2004)

I wish it thought me
worthy to linger in
the light of the gates
I wish the seraph in
the purple skirt or
the archangel-boy in the tight jeans
found nobility enough in me
for the night to never cease

because in that night
God's name in her native language
was on my hips

[1]see every single American teen or new adult drama film since the
1980s

tempting my echo of its swaying syllabisms
never illegible
but forever unpronounceable

critical-level performance of the rite
has apocalyptic properties—
that is, both provably destructive
and with great potential to induce
prophecy

the music did hit me
and your body did catch me
and somewhere in the centre
of those competing gravities
was the cosmos in its own waistline motion
lover, your bumper bring meh back
to the first time meh mudda
call meh name . . .

at a terminal velocity, surviving
subjects have documented a shared
awakening, with potential to span miles
of air or sea[2], lingering within the senses
as stored rhapsodic biodata, an open-circuit
physical ecstasy and a redundant
rotational climax

under closed eyes
the shadow of the world does turn bright
hot on the faces of the next world war
and warm on the hands that halt it
I done sail across the black in this wine
take large swallows from the swirling nebula of it
lust as its nucleus

[2]evidence of distance-resistant wining effects have been well documented in Japan; see 'Japanese Wine' (Minmi 2008), 'Kanpai Wine' (Barbie Japan 2009), 'Wine For Me' (Rudebwoy Face 2009)

opens my eyes to star-birth, star-death,
the warmth of your hot celestial body[3]

this euphoric quality is known to be
intensely addictive at even average
potentials, especially for men. It should however be
noted that excessive wining
can be destructive to the recipient (Machel
Montano 2012), even inducing animalistic
transformations in male recipients
(Anslem Douglas 1998). Also, coercion or other
non-consensual gyratory communions
are discouraged, not only for their
lack of energy potential, but their
ability to harm performers,
severing their connection to the
enthusiasmos; the power of the
ritual is placed firmly in the waist
of the oracle (Patrice Roberts 2014, Alison Hinds 2005)

if I could stay drowning in the syrup-sugary-smooth
sway of your silhouette 'til sunrise
God knows I would die against your body
but the Holy Spirit does only give you
the Pentecost that you could handle
so you step away with a wink
to join your crew for drinks
gates to abounding knowledge closed again

until some soca
draws them golden open
for someone luckier than
me

[3]a peculiar star rich in copper with an orbit too fast and fierce for a
rock like me to not erode in its power

time, and time again

long before our time:
we were forbidden gentlemen,
sneaking held hands under coats
and hiding love's passwords
in simple sentences.
my heart is a hummingbird
and your lips
are sweet as a hibiscus—

tuesday:
I wear the only suit I have,
you bought it for me because
my own was loose and moth-bit.
the morning's speckled with sorry-for-your-losses
and your sister mutters at the wake
that God would've kept you
if you didn't love me
and I don't know if I disagree
and I can't forget the sight
of you, restful, in your last bed.
I want to be wrapped up in you
and hear you whisper
'don't forget you owe me
a kiss in the morning' one
more—

wednesday:
in another universe
I get up
and pay my debt
you get up
and collect
in another universe
I take that other me's place
and you are still sweet,
as sweet as the crash never happened,
hands living-warm against my cheeks
when you ask,

'come on, baby boy,
why you cryin'?'—

friday:
I have tried to find
the space and time
when you still are.
the curtains have been drawn
in the living room since the funeral.
your mother brought brown rum
and lasagna
and tears to my eyes,
said no lover has never been in your corner
as long as I have.
I let slip that I'm still hoping
that you get up before death counts ten
and give life a wicked left hook.
you still owe me a
blasted kiss—

monday:
for a gasp of afternoon
I am when you are.
I don't stop crying,
crying 'I miss you, man',
and I stop trying to hide it
and you stop asking
because I kiss you like a
glutton. time won't even
let me have you for
six minutes, but the air
next to the dining table
still smells like my sweet hibiscus boy—

sunday:
by now, it's become
a given. I step between
two worlds, and just
one knows you. on the
other's anniversary of burial,
you run your hands through

my hair, and I pay
dozens of arrears you don't know about
with interest
like it will buy your body back
from the earth—

long after our time:
soon time will grow
bored and cast us in
some other dollhouse drama.
you ever wonder which?
star-crossed spies? partners-in-crime?
or are our roles so honed
that I can stay the eager clumsy hummingbird
at some stiff house party
bouncing from wallflower to wallflower
'til I rest my lips on you?

tuesday:
you owe me
my blasted kiss.
do you hear me say it?

tar baby

I figure there's a
story about this already,
but mine's a little
different:

there he is, glistening dark,
skin congealing of crude,
taunting me wide-eyed
long-tongued.

He's just like his father, the carelessness that
birthed him, so rude, fingers on everything he can see,
swallowing the whole world whole, all his skin a mouth,
effortless.

How does the earth plan to get herself out of this
sticky situation? Will there be a next
episode of this drama, or a same time, or a same
channel?

The foxes wanted something to eat, after all.
To roast it all and grin, to live rich at the summit.
But the smoke rose to meet them. The tar baby never
stopped

hungering. It already ate all of the poor.
That was just its job. Its salary was
the flesh of everything else.

That Business They Call Utopia, Part Three

The vines will think they are veins.
They will try to eat the alabaster pillars
—mind, I have no particular attachment to those pillars,
yet still—
and its pillowed places will fill up with brambles
—mind, I don't care about the comfort of those inside,
yet still—
and when you try to cut them, they will shout,
'what about the lawn, turning lush, hiding stones?
you would rob us of a chance to rise up like them?'
And maybe someone will even say it builds character,
bulbs of ichor pooling in its guts. It shows its true heart.
Maybe some very cleansing organ waits to beat inside.
Here's the contemptuous truth:
riot is a fertilizer, but some things prefer to grow
out of the flesh of better neighbors.
Yea, even rosiest vines will weed. Especially those.
Their roots gather apostemes, and gullible creatures drink.
What about the kinder tree, lost as this violence
rushed to cast bruise-shadows on freedom's old stones?
Well, you say, at least the walls are clean.

Lovecraft Thesis #4

(*'Lockdown'* [*Radio Edit*])

At the anthills of acrimony
form brick-red rivers of magma to curse
the lost. They cannot seem to withstand
the slowly shambling thought that a people
in pain would wail. When the asphalt
becomes a singular novel cry, when the
bank building glass gives way to unlearned language,
they will trap themselves in their homes,
they will have revelatory trysts with their guns,
they will proclaim a broken sky full of gods of
destruction from beyond to eat the world.
And will that not be bizarre?
Fear will make them beseech steel idols, make
them tribute tin emblems of their own force,
make them remake the past itself just to sleep
past the din of incomprehensible prayer
chanting under the nearest streetlight.
And will that not reveal that
they are broken by what they've learnt?
They will struggle to forget that
if they seek to trap
a thing they worry will undo all the reality
they've worked so hard to steal, or blot out
the sound of truths too deep to fathom before it
ruins their ever-patient minds, then it is because
the neighbours they have refused

are as gods to them.

Lovecraft Thesis #5

(*Visions of Bodies Being Burned*, Track 6)

The man you say brought us here is a kind of prophet.
He saw the cloaks along the shoreline,
knew the foul faith deep within their threads.
Such powerful irony, then, to share a
tone of voice with those hooded shadows,
men who call themselves warlocks of a pure truth
they could never read. Ever notice
how they huddle around warped symbols,
pledge fealty to idols long since dust,
march on wearing capsized ideas
on their heads to hide from sight?
They hope some twisted nature will reveal
deserved kingdom, will let any void
glimpse them if they'll have it, slip on
monstrous shapes they call heritage
and drift through the earth like wind-snatched
kite paper. And for what?
What else than to own the carcass
of a land already bought in blood?

That Business They Call Utopia, Part One

How it works, it seems,
is that there is this sharp-shelled
and bitter seed that digs its root
into the fine soft soil, strangles the edges
of our very normal want to eat
and not be torn to pieces, and sets its pistils
upward to the heat of a rage
so it can grow its barbs.

They apparently scatter all
on their own, shaken off the muddy
shoes of the big town pastor
and finding a spot in your lawn
so it can pick at the ankles of neighbors
and try to polish its petals foil-colored,

and if you have enough,
like maybe a few hundred in their potted seats
in a stadium somewhere willing to pick at themselves,
you can turn the sand beneath them into enough one-way glass
to force the sun in every direction
into the eyes of mothers
whose names you do not know
and hope they crumble under their sweat,

so there's a whole racket now, of sowing them
everywhere till folks call it a common sight,
till it busts through the concrete outside your boy's high school,
till it catches the blood from my brother's torn cheek and shimmers,
till its faintest trichomes try to pull the strings from my thigh
so it can get at my head better.

I hear the easy way's to check your gardens
often to see the spites sprout from the dirt,
a stern pluck delivered early before the sun warms it.
But barring that, once it's run your whole yard,
taken your loveliest flowers in its ideology,
ask yourself: how do you want your lawn to be seen?

drop some amens

The Holy Barons rumble through
the untended slum-gardens against the highway
and drop payloads.
If the halo-copters hear you scream from downstairs,

you get one from on high, and it makes
a whistle on the way down and

falls against your prayers—
it goes through one girl's bedroom ceiling

and suddenly her college first-pick
knows how to spell her name,

writes it on a very eager letter to her mother;
it falls over the edge of the general hospital

and my neighbor can breathe without burning
through the bullet wound;

bam over the house on the hill
and she can afford to fix her eye

in Iceland without having to beg;
and *bam* in the river on the other side

and no more coughs or cholera
in the news the next morning;

and *bam* wins a granny the lottery one week
so she can keep her lonely son clean;

and *bam* loses an uncle the lottery the next
so he can keep his lonely heart clean;

and against the stained glass
for more baptisms than burials;

and against the muzzles
of things lost in the street

for less bad news than
boys made new.

I don't know who calls in the coordinates,
where the map's pushpin pricks turn into precipitation

but god, look at the damage littering this place.
It's spare, and rare, but cratering,

changing people's whole lives
with one whisper of gravity.

I just wish one day one of those
prayer-bombs could fall on me.

Acknowledgments

A thousand thanks to the editors and staff of the following publications which have housed these works:

Uncanny Magazine:
"Birth, Place"
"the one"
"time, and time again"
"drop some amens"

Arsenika:
"the lagahoo speaks for itself"
"The Metaphysics of a Wine, in Theory and Practice"

Sunvault:
"The Sailor-Boys"

Thank you to my family, especially my mother, Sandra, whose support of my work has refused to waver.

Thank you to my local poetry family, especially Deneka Thomas, Shivanee Ramlochan, Derron Sandy, and Arielle John, whose constant striving and dedication to outreach through the word has motivated me on more than one occasion.

Thank you to Karen Lord, without whose mentorship I may not have even sold my first speculative anything. Your guidance and thoughtfulness is a constant inspiration.

Thank you to my speculative poetry family, especially Fran Wilde, who has cast her magical eye on many of the pieces in this collection. Thanks again to Fran, and to Sara Norja, Karolina Fedyk, C.S.E. Cooney, Cassandra Khaw, S. Qiouyi Lu, R.B. Lemberg, Bogi Takács, Ali Trotta, Hester J. Rook, and so many others, whose friendship, conversation, and verse have been overwhelmingly encouraging.

Thank you to Holly Lyn Walrath and Saba Syed Razvi for selecting this collection, and again to Holly for being a strong poetic inspiration even before this selection. Thank you to proofreaders Sydney Richardson and Elliot Brooks for their diligent attention to making these poems the best they can be.

Thank you, reader—not only for reading this, but for diving into the starlight pool of verse at all. Thank you for resting your eyes here.

Author's Note

In mid-2018, I once submitted to one of my favorite science fiction and fantasy magazines a poem I had written mostly on a lark—a semi-comic juxtaposition between the weird, surreal, often hostile relationship the media has with one particular musician and actor, and the similarly weird, surreal, hostile lens through which one of science fiction's most beloved mythologies would view that same person based solely on their body. To be quite honest, the poem was a very sudden thing, the stuff of poetic genius that wiser artists remark on—or wiser poets warn you against—all the time. I had written it months before almost as an experiment. In that year, I had read it aloud only once. Beyond that, I hadn't thought about that poem much more that day.

Four months later, accountant Botham Jean was shot dead in his apartment by a Dallas Police Department patrol officer who came off the wrong floor in her apartment building. She found a non-threatening, surely afraid Jean, in his own living room, eating ice cream, not expecting to face a police-issue pistol that evening, and she took his life for alleged fear of her own.

This juxtaposition surely means very little to most. Sadly, a death of a Black person by extrajudicial police violence seems to be a punctuating event in the international calendar—even if you can't set your watch to it, you know where you were when it happened, its relation in time to other moments in your life. I am not an American citizen, but things stood out to me regardless: he was born in the Caribbean, a St. Lucian citizen; he was only a few years younger than me, an accountant with one of the States' most popular firms. In short, in a lot of the ways many other Black people point out that someone has worked very hard to not deserve this kind of violence, it still visited Jean at a moment he could not prepare for.

One of science fiction's most well-known authors has a history in his work of devaluing and denigrating people of colour.

We don't need to go into the details. I suspect that you know. If you've gotten this far in the collection, at least you can proffer a guess. It obviously wasn't his claim to fame—he was an otherwise talented and creative hand in the genre, and we credit him on the expansion of an entire subgenre mythos that science fantasy and horror still reveres to this day.

The conversation is a challenging, bitter thing: it would be utterly dishonest to say that the creator in question hasn't had a strong, indelible effect on the genre, and yet that effect is shaped by an undeniable, hostile fear. Far wiser persons have already observed how the core themes of the Cthulhu mythos—of unfathomable knowledge rendering mortals catatonic with fear and madness as they gaze upon creatures they can barely use words to define—share so much, at least superficially, with the same mindset that powers old-school racial discrimination—a fear of the unknown, a suspicion of the intentions of others, and a misguided feeling of superiority. Hell, the name that the creator in question (or one of his parents) gave to his childhood pet cat is a silently repeated meme on social media as we speak.

Does it bear repeating that the caliber of racism he espoused in his heyday of the 1910s to 1930s was not uncommon among white Americans? Of course—but it would be a sorry excuse, as if to imply racism was some unavoidable product of circumstance rather than the deliberate ideology of spiteful people, some of whom may be honestly otherwise remarkable (much to the benefit of that spite). There is no shame or cruelty in observing this. He was a truly remarkable creative mind, but one whose creativity was colored by a misguided value of monoculturalism.

Science fiction is a radical genre, but that fact is a neutral one. It has the capacity to unlock the anxieties of today and cast them back to us through a myriad of lenses, some so clinical and precise that the tiniest flecks of complexity appear in sharp relief, others so comically absurd that as you watch you cannot help but ask aloud, "do we really behave like that? Damn. That's… weird, isn't it?" Sometimes the thing you see on the other end of that lens is that we think that we mean so much to the universe, are so rare and special to it, that we would never be able to deal with the fact that we are truly so insignificant that leviathans larger than our philosophy are acting out their own strange drama without even noticing that we're there, too small to them to even be pests.

But in there is an even more interesting counterpoint: sometimes the lens shows us that there are creatures—people—who think themselves so perfect and incontrovertible in the face of something so small and seemingly worthless that they never notice exactly how resourceful, how resilient, and how significant we may be.

In mid-2016, the experimental hip hop group clipping. released their second studio album, *Splendor & Misery.* Just under a year later, it was nominated for a Hugo Award in the Best Dramatic Presentation (Short Form) category, although it sadly didn't win. It is one of only three music records to be nominated for a Dramatic Presentation Hugo in the history of the overall category, and the first time a recorded album had been so nominated since 1971. Two such nominations are theirs—in 2018, the band would score another such nomination for their single 'The Deep'.

The Bandcamp description of *Splendor & Misery* describes it in part as "a reversal of H.P. Lovecraft's concept of cosmic insignificance", wherein the protagonist of the Afrofuturist concept album "finds relief in learning that humanity is of no consequence to the vast, uncaring universe". Instead of being scandalized by the revelation that he is small in such a neverending space, that feeling is freeing—he is unbound by what the notion denies. There is a radical unlocking in discovering that, on a supreme level, no mortal is superior or inferior to you, the universe doesn't owe you or anyone else anything, and every piece of you, for good or for ill, will turn to dust in its wake and the breadth of it will never notice. There is nothing maddening about being small, the album argues. In fact, it mostly clearly reveals the hollowness of man's inhumanity to man, and to the marginalised in particular.

This is not the only work that has taken the most recognizable parts of the Cthulhu mythos and reshaped them for thoughtful and critical effect. From the most deliberate reimaginings of Victor LaValle's *The Ballad of Black Tom* and Matt Ruff's *Lovecraft Country* to even the admonishing context written into the rules document of the *Fate of Cthulhu* tabletop roleplaying game, we have acknowledged how resilient the mythos is as a subgenre of horror, and from where it emerged in the author's mind, and have cast that lens back inward to the work with incredible effect.

The end goal of this collection is in the same spirit as those works, but hoping to accomplish the inverse: for Blackness to be seen as radically significant.

It is. It has no choice but to be. It has spent the better part of the history of the old New World being significant enough to be the driver of entire industries of capital, the metaphorical and literal masons of entire nations, the driven bodies of decades of conflict, torture, struggle, exile, revolution, and resilience, and has survived throughout.

One may imagine that, if there were an entity so large and unfathomable that it looked past such centuries as if they were mere moments, it would still be impressed at how many moments there have been, and how brutal they have been—but also how filled with hard-fought pride, resistance, declaration, and joy. To hazard a tired analogy, even if we were as ants to such gods, you would imagine they respond the same as we do when we learn that ants can carry so many times their own weight, and withstand forces many times more still—with a kind of childish awe that they would resist, even in the face of such an unbending world.

The truth of our world is much like the truth of clipping's album—all over the world, Black people have witnessed vast and indefatigable systems built specifically for us to struggle to grasp them, so deep and cruel that they tell us to our face how small we're meant to feel, so unmoving that the act of challenging them is meant to drive us wild with rage or sorrow. And yet, not only have we stood our ground in the face of those systems, we have survived them, we have lived in the face of them, we strove to understand them, and finally many of us actually touched those systems with our own hands. And even though those elder beings—the law, the medical practice, the police, housing, employment, the faith, and so much more—are still so cantankerous that they may wrestle violently in our grip, never content to take our understanding for power, at least so many of our siblings did still earn that knowledge. In struggling against those monsters, they have won, at least, the understanding that there is nothing truly special about them—and simultaneously, even in our utter banality, a world of wonder about how we've made it this far.

Admittedly, a large portion of that intent is also to make you laugh. Just because someone is significant doesn't mean there is no room for them to be imperfect, and in that imperfection I try to find spaces where something truer than praise, and yet lighter than shame, can be found. Not everyone who writes an autograph in this collection is good or right all of the time, and not all of the circumstances under which they are asked to sign are good or right at their immediate moments. That's fine. We spend so much time struggling under the weight of how the media 'perfectly' sees Blackness—one moment perfectly broken and untrustworthy, the station of the poor and downtrodden who live to rob or hurt you, and then the next moment perfectly talented and accomplished, always willing to bear unnecessary burdens for free to prove their worth. Sometimes, though, we're just tired, hungry, selfish, mistaken, distracted. Sometimes we are not in the mood.

The resilience for which we credit having survived such a cruel universe for so long, I reckon, has nothing to do with being perfect, unbreakable, or just. It is neutral fact. We are here because we have made an effort to remain, and to value what remains, as we must. But I think it's also worth remembering that we can do so without it being perfect—that we can be given the paradoxical gift of being valued because we have survived being insignificant with such undeniable magnitude.

About the Author

Brandon O'Brien is a writer, performance poet, teaching artist and game designer from Trinidad and Tobago. His work has been shortlisted for the 2014 Alice Yard Prize for Art Writing, the 2014 and 2015 Small Axe Literary Competitions, and the inaugural Ignyte Award for Best Speculative Poetry. His work is published in *Uncanny Magazine*, *Strange Horizons*, *Reckoning*, and *New Worlds, Old Ways: Speculative Tales from the Caribbean*, among others. He is the former Poetry editor of *FIYAH: A Magazine of Black Speculative Fiction.*

About the Cover Artist

Trevor Fraley is an illustrator with a passion for characters and the worlds that they inhabit. Starting at a young age, he was always interested in the ability to tell stories through a visual medium. Throughout years of exposure to countless mediums from storybooks, film, television and many others, the idea of creating impactful work from seemingly thin air drove him to pursue this endeavor.

In 2016 he earned his BFA in Illustration from the University of the Arts in Philadelphia where he also received the Marcel Vertes Award. Since then his work has been featured in numerous outlets such as Medium, FIYAH Magazine, Action Lab Comics and Silverclutch Games.

Trevor continues to add to the world of illustration while also finding new and intriguing ways to contribute to the world that we live in.

Interstellar Flight Press

Interstellar Flight Press is an indie speculative publishing house. We feature innovative works from the best new writers in science fiction and fantasy. In the words of Ursula K. Le Guin, we need "writers who can see alternatives to how we live now, can see through our fear-stricken society and its obsessive technologies to other ways of being, and even imagine real grounds for hope."

Find us online at www.interstellarflightpress.com.